TOP 10 PHYSICALLY CHALLENGED ATHLETES

Jeff Savage

SPORTS TOP 10

Enslow Publishers, Inc.

40 Industrial Road   PO Box 38
Box 398   Aldershot
Berkeley Heights, NJ 07922   Hants GU12 6BP
USA   UK

http://www.enslow.com

Library of Congress Cataloging-in-Publication Data

Savage, Jeff, 1961–
    Top 10 physically challenged athletes / Jeff Savage.
        p. cm. — (Sports top 10)
    Includes bibliographical references and index.
    Summary: Profiles ten physically challenged athletes in sports history, including Jim Abbott, Three Finger Brown, and Wilma Rudolph.
    ISBN 0-7660-1272-7
    1. Physically handicapped athletes—United States Biography Juvenile literature. 2. Physically handicapped athletes—Rating of—United States Juvenile literature. [1. Athletes. 2. Physically handicapped.] I. Title. II. Title: Top ten physically challenged athletes. III. Series.
GV697.A1S33   2000
796'.087'092273—dc21
[B]   99-15901
                                            CIP

Printed in the United States of America

10 9 8 7 6 5 4 3 2 1

To Our Readers: All Internet addresses in this book were active and appropriate when we went to press. Any comments or suggestions can be sent by e-mail to Comments@enslow.com or to the address on the back cover.

Illustration Credits: Amateur Athletic Foundation of Los Angeles, pp. 30, 33, 39; © New Orleans Saints, p. 19; © The United States Golf Association, pp. 26, 29; © The United States Golf Association, John Mummert, pp. 34, 37; ERIC LARS BAKKE, pp. 42, 45; INTELESYS, p. 21; NATIONAL BASEBALL HALL OF FAME LIBRARY, COOPERSTOWN, N.Y., pp. 10, 13, 14, 17, 23, 25; Ron Vesely–Chicago White Sox, p. 6; Tennessee State University, p. 41; University of Michigan, p. 9.

Cover Illustration: © The United States Golf Association, John Mummert

Cover Description: Casey Martin, professional golfer.

Interior Design: Richard Stalzer

CONTENTS

Introduction

THE ODDS OF BECOMING A PROFESSIONAL athlete are slim. Millions of young people play sports, many with dreams of reaching the top. But only a few dozen each year actually make it. Athletes with physical challenges play sports, too, and they share the same dreams as everyone else.

Strength, speed, quickness, agility, endurance, and hand-eye coordination are all qualities that determine an athlete's success. A weakness in any of these areas might mean the difference between playing sports for a living and playing just for fun. That is why the odds are even longer for a person with a physical disability to become a pro. They must do what others do *and* overcome their disabilities.

Baseball pitchers need their hands, don't they? Well, Jim Abbott was born without a right hand. But he did not let that stop him from becoming a major-league pitcher. Mordecai Brown was known as "Three- Finger" for just that reason, but he used his disability to his advantage on the mound. Grover Cleveland Alexander suffered from double vision, hearing loss, and seizures, yet he was among the greatest pitchers in history. Baseball hitters certainly need their arms to swing the bat, don't they? Pete Gray has only one arm, but he reached the major leagues. Just as baseball pitchers would seem to need their hands and batters their arms, football kickers need their foot, right? Tom Dempsey was born with half a foot, yet he used that foot to kick the longest field goal in National Football League (NFL) history. Golfers walk about six miles in a normal round of 18 holes. Ben Hogan survived a violent car crash and nearly lost the use of his legs. Yet he achieved many more victories. Likewise, Casey Martin has overcome a birth defect in his leg to play pro golf. For track-and-field athletes who require endurance, there is no more important organ in the body than the lungs. Jackie Joyner-Kersee overcame asthma to become the greatest heptathlete in track history. Likewise, for sprinters, nothing is more important than their legs. Wilma Rudolph's leg was paralyzed when she was a child and she spent years in a metal brace, yet she became the "World's Fastest Woman." Football, more than any other sport, is one of noises. It is important to hear the coaches, the play calls in the huddle, the signals at the scrimmage line. Yet Kenny Walker became a pro lineman despite being deaf.

What does it take for someone with a disability to become a great athlete? First, it takes the courage to try. The fear of failure must be overcome by the attempt to play the sport. Next, it takes practice. Finally, it takes perseverance. With the odds stacked against them, challenged athletes must try even harder than everyone else. These athletes possessed the inner drive it took to excel at their sport. There have been other great physically challenged athletes, so choosing just ten was not easy to do. Perhaps you can think of others. In the meantime, here is *our* list.

PHYSICALLY CHALLENGED ATHLETES

ATHLETE	SPORT
JIM ABBOTT	BASEBALL
GROVER CLEVELAND ALEXANDER	BASEBALL
MORDECAI BROWN	BASEBALL
TOM DEMPSEY	FOOTBALL
PETE GRAY	BASEBALL
BEN HOGAN	GOLF
JACKIE JOYNER-KERSEE	TRACK AND FIELD
CASEY MARTIN	GOLF
WILMA RUDOLPH	TRACK AND FIELD
KENNY WALKER	FOOTBALL

JIM ABBOTT

Jim Abbott, who was born without a right hand, pitched an amazing no-hitter against the Cleveland Indians at Yankee Stadium in 1993.

JIM ABBOTT

JIM ABBOTT HAS NO RIGHT HAND. So he stood on the mound at Yankee Stadium in New York and used his left hand to throw pitches past the hitters. It was late in the 1993 season, and Abbott was weaving his magic once again. One by one he was sending the Cleveland Indians muttering back to their dugout. Abbott didn't stop until he had pitched all nine innings without allowing a run or a hit. Pitching a no-hitter in the major leagues is amazing enough; doing it with just one hand seems like a miracle.

James Anthony Abbott was born with a right arm that stopped at the wrist. He was teased at school and told his stubbed hand looked more like a foot. When he was five, his parents, Mike and Kathy, had a doctor fit him with an artificial hand called a prosthesis. The teasing grew worse. Jim's parents let him quit wearing the prosthesis after six months.

Abbott enjoyed playing sports. He was encouraged to focus on soccer because his disability would not hinder him in a game. But he loved baseball. So his father helped him learn to throw and field the ball with the same hand. As he delivered the pitch, he balanced his glove on his right wrist, then slipped the glove on his left hand. After fielding the ball, he tucked the glove under his right arm. He reached in with his left hand to grab the ball and make the throw. He practiced the awkward movements for hours a day by throwing against a wall, and eventually he could do it all in the blink of an eye. It became known as the Great Abbott Switch.

Jim Abbott pitched his first game at age eleven in Little

League and threw a no-hitter. In high school he had to prove himself over and over again. In one game his freshman year, a team had its first eight batters try to reach base by bunting on him. The first batter reached base safely. Abbott threw out the next seven. He earned a scholarship to the University of Michigan, where he combined with another pitcher for a no-hitter in his first home start. A year later he made Team USA and became the ace of the staff. In the 1988 Olympics in Seoul, South Korea, he pitched the United States over Japan in the gold-medal game. "My dream of a lifetime," he called it.[1]

Abbott was drafted in the first round by the California Angels in 1988. He became just the ninth player in twenty-five years to skip the minor leagues and play his first pro game at the major-league level. He won 12 games as a starter his first year. That was the most wins by an Angels rookie in sixteen years. He received so many fan letters that the Angels had to keep his mail in shopping carts. His best season came in 1991 when he went 18–11 with a 2.89 earned run average (ERA) and finished third in the voting for the American League Cy Young Award. He retired in 1997, but then made a comeback in 1998. Pitching for the Chicago White Sox that year, Abbott went 5–0, with a 4.55 ERA. Prior to the 1999 season, Abbott signed a contract to pitch for the Milwaukee Brewers, but was released in mid-season. He retired from baseball on July 27 of that year.

Abbott's story of courage still inspires thousands. "When an obstacle of any kind pops up in your life, don't sit down and give up," Abbott explains. "You just have to keep on trying and one day it will pay off. People who aren't afraid to meet a challenge are the real heroes in my book."[2]

JIM ABBOTT

SPORT: Baseball.

BORN: September 19, 1967, Flint, Michigan.

HIGH SCHOOL: Flint Central High School, Flint, Michigan.

COLLEGE: University of Michigan.

PRO: California Angels, 1989–1992, 1995–1996; New York Yankees, 1993–1994; Chicago White Sox, 1995, 1998; Milwaukee Brewers, 1999.

ACHIEVEMENTS: Pitched gold-medal game victory vs. Japan at Olympic Games, 1988; pitched no-hitter vs. Cleveland Indians, 1993.

HONORS: Golden Spikes Award (best amateur baseball player), 1987; Sullivan Award (best amateur athlete), 1987; First-team All-America, 1988.

When he was drafted by the California Angels, Jim Abbott became one of a small number of players who skipped the minor leagues and played his first professional game at the major-league level.

Internet Address

http://www.milwaukeebrewers.com/media/1996bios/abbott.html

GROVER CLEVELAND ALEXANDER

As a result of fighting in World War I, Grover Cleveland Alexander suffered from epilepsy. He refused to let the disease prevent him from playing baseball at a Hall of Fame level.

GROVER CLEVELAND ALEXANDER

GROVER CLEVELAND ALEXANDER WAS HIS TEAM'S last hope. Manager Rogers Hornsby handed him the baseball and said, "Well, the bases are full. Lazzeri's up, and there ain't no place to put him."[1] It was Game 7 of the 1926 World Series. The St. Louis Cardinals were clinging to a 3–2 lead over the mighty New York Yankees. "Yeah, well," Alexander said as he took the ball, "I guess I'll have to take care of him then."[2]

Yankee Stadium was rocking as Tony Lazzeri stepped into the box. Alexander had pitched a complete game the day before to win Game 6, his second complete game victory of the Series. He had done that despite suffering from several illnesses. Now he was being asked to save this game in relief. Did he have any strength left? With barely a windup, Alexander threw the first pitch low for ball one. He came back with a strike to even the count. His next pitch was whacked by Lazzeri down the line—just foul. Working quickly, Alexander came in with the next pitch, a curve low and outside, and Lazzeri swung and missed for strike three. Alexander worked out of the jam. But the Cards had not won their first World Series just yet. First, Alexander set down the Yankees in order in the eighth. Then in the ninth, he got the first two outs, before walking Babe Ruth. But Ruth was caught stealing for the last out, giving St. Louis the title.

Grover Cleveland Alexander was born in Elba, Nebraska, and grew up in nearby St. Paul. After completing high school, he pitched in the minors. He joined the major-league Philadelphia Phillies in 1911, and made his first start against the world champion Philadelphia A's in an exhibition game at the tiny Baker Bowl. "You'll pitch five innings," catcher Pat Moran told him. "They'll be murder, but you'll learn something."[3] Instead, Moran and his teammates learned they had a star when Alexander pitched five innings of perfect baseball, allowing no runs, hits, or walks.

Alexander had to pitch in the Baker Bowl bandbox—another term for a small stadium. Its tin fence in right field was only 290 feet from the plate. Alexander won an amazing 28 games pitching there his rookie year, including a 12-inning, one-hit, 1–0 shutout over Cy Young. Then came an amazing three-year stretch starting in 1915 in which he won 31, 33, and 30 games. Babe Ruth said that with Alexander pitching "the fellow who was up there at the plate with a bat on his shoulder felt like a sucker."[4]

The Phillies feared Alexander would be lost to the U.S. Army for World War I, so they traded him to the Cubs. Sure enough, he pitched in just three games for the Cubs before joining the army. As a sergeant for a field artillery unit in France, he was gassed on the battlefield. He also lost his hearing in one ear from the constant sound of bombs exploding. He had already been afflicted with double vision from a minor-league accident years earlier. After he returned home from the war, he began to suffer fits and seizures in which his body shook uncontrollably because he now had the disease known as epilepsy.

He refused to let the disease stop him from playing baseball. Alexander won 27 games in 1920, and 22 more in 1923. In all, he won 128 games for Chicago alone. In 1926, he was traded to the Cardinals, where he led them to the World Series title. He retired with a career record of 373 wins and just 208 losses, and took a job in a flea circus. Later, he worked in Times Square in New York City, where people paid a nickel each to listen to him tell the story of the day he struck out Lazzeri.

GROVER CLEVELAND ALEXANDER

SPORT: Baseball.

BORN: February 26, 1887, Elba, Nebraska.

DIED: November 4, 1950.

HIGH SCHOOL: St. Paul High School, St. Paul, Nebraska.

PRO: Philadelphia Phillies, 1911–1917, 1930; Chicago Cubs, 1918–1926; St. Louis Cardinals, 1926–1929.

RECORDS: Tied for most career wins (373) in National League; holds record for most shutouts in a season (16), 1916; ranks second in career shutouts (90).

HONORS: National Baseball Hall of Fame, 1938.

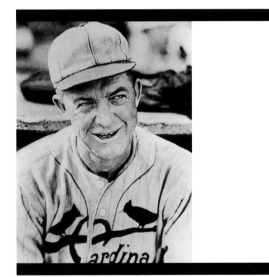 

Despite epilepsy, deafness in one ear, and double vision, Alexander led the St. Louis Cardinals to the 1926 World Series championship. He retired from baseball with a career record of 373 wins and 208 losses.

Internet Address

http://www.baseballhalloffame.org/members/hofers/gca/gca.html

MORDECAI BROWN

Mordecai "Three-Finger" Brown earned his nickname after he injured his right hand in two separate incidents as a small boy. His injuries may have helped him as a pitcher.

MORDECAI BROWN

THE FANS FILLED THE POLO GROUNDS in New York so fast that the gates were closed an hour before the game. Thousands more sat on a hill called Coogan's Bluff above the field. They were there to see legendary pitcher Christy Mathewson and his New York Giants play the Chicago Cubs for the 1908 pennant. Right away, the first five Giants reached base in the first inning, producing two runs, and the New York fans figured the game was theirs. Cubs starter Jack Pfiester was removed from the game at that point, and a new pitcher stepped onto the mound for Chicago. It was Mordecai "Three-Finger" Brown. It spelled trouble for the Giants.

Christy Mathewson had thrown a no-hitter against Brown early in the 1905 season. From that day on, over the next four years, Brown had Mathewson's and the Giants' number. Three-Finger beat Mathewson nine straight times. This game was the last of the nine. Three-Finger shut out the Giants on four hits the rest of the way, and the Cubs scored four times in the third inning to win the game, 4–2, and take the pennant.

Brown's full name was Mordecai Peter Centennial Brown. At age seven, he caught his right hand in a corn shredder on his uncle's Indiana farm. That caused him to lose all but an inch of his index finger and the use of his little finger. A few weeks later, with his injured hand in a cast, he broke his third and fourth fingers when he fell while chasing a hog. Those fingers healed into a gnarled shape.

But Brown's crippled hand turned out to be an advantage. He was working as a coal miner and playing third base in the minor leagues when his team's pitcher fell and injured his shoulder. Who can pitch around here, the coach wondered? Brown gave it a try. As he baffled the hitters, he surprised everyone, including himself. The ball sliding off his three fingers turned into either a natural sinker ball or a wicked curve. A pitcher was born. The St. Louis Cardinals signed him in 1903. He won nine games for the Cards his rookie year, but was foolishly traded to the Cubs after the season. Starting in 1906, he won 20 games or more for the Cubs in six straight seasons.

In 1907, Ty Cobb bragged that he would hit .800 against the Cubs in the World Series. Brown held Cobb to one hit in four at bats. Three-Finger was a superb fielder as well, with cat-quick feet and soft hands. In 1908, he fielded 108 balls without committing an error. Even more impressive that year, he won 29 games, a Cubs record that may never be broken. In 1911 he had another remarkable season, completing 21 of the 27 games he started, winning 16 of them, and also recording 13 saves. While he was starring for the Cubs, the corn shredder that damaged his hand was put on display for tourists in his rural Indiana hometown.

Brown was a brilliant pitcher, but those who knew him said he was an even better person. "There never was a finer character," said teammate Johnny Evers. "He was charitable and friendly to his foes and ever willing to help a youngster breaking in."[1]

MORDECAI BROWN

Sᴘᴏʀᴛ: Baseball.

Bᴏʀɴ: October 19, 1876, Nyesville, Indiana.

Dɪᴇᴅ: February 14, 1948.

Pʀᴏ: St. Louis Cardinals, 1903; Chicago Cubs, 1904–1912, 1916; Cincinnati Reds, 1913; St. Louis Terriers, 1914; Brooklyn Brookfeds, 1914; Chicago Whales, 1915.

Sᴛᴀᴛs: Holds Cubs team record for most wins in a season (29); ranks third all-time in the majors in career earned run average (2.06).

Hᴏɴᴏʀs: National Baseball Hall of Fame, 1949.

Brown was a great fielder as well as a top-notch pitcher. In 1908, he won a team-record 29 games for the Chicago Cubs.

Internet Address

http://www.baseballhalloffame.org/members/hofers/mpcb/mpcb.html

TOM DEMPSEY

THE ODDS WERE AGAINST HIM, but Tom Dempsey had overcome poor odds his whole life. The New Orleans Saints were asking Dempsey to kick a 63-yard field goal. Never mind that Dempsey was born with only half a foot. He could kick with his special leather boot. But 63 yards? No kicker in the history of pro football had ever made one longer than 56 yards.

Dempsey trotted onto the field at Tulane Stadium in New Orleans, Louisiana, with two seconds left and his team trailing the Detroit Lions, 17–16. Dempsey's Saints had not won a game the entire 1970 season. Their coach had been fired just days before. When new coach J. D. Roberts sent his kicker onto the field, the Lions expected a trick play.

Holder Joe Scarpati crouched into position. Dempsey looked up at the goal posts and saw them far away. "I knew it was a long field goal," said Dempsey. "I never counted the distance. If I'd have counted 63 yards, I would have probably choked."[1] The ball was snapped and spotted, and the Lions made a half-hearted attempt to rush in, figuring this was some sort of joke. Dempsey whipped his leg through and thumped the ball skyward. It sailed high and far through the air and didn't come down until it had cleared the crossbar. Dempsey had done it. Almost thirty years later, this field goal remained etched in the NFL's record book tied for the longest ever.

Tom Dempsey was born with half a right foot and no right hand. As a boy growing up in California, he underwent sixteen operations on his arm and foot. He was teased at school and often came home crying. Tom's father spent

TOM DEMPSEY

Tom Dempsey, born with half a right foot and no right hand, kicked an amazing 63-yard field goal in 1970.

many nights trying to convince his son that he was "normal." Tom trusted his father enough to try out for sports. He played on his high school football and wrestling teams, then became a 260-pound star defensive end at Palomar Junior College in southern California. He learned to kick in college and tried out for the San Diego Chargers in 1968 but was cut from the team. He joined the Saints in 1969 and finished among the NFL scoring leaders that season, making the Pro Bowl as a rookie. The following year, he made his record-breaking kick.

Then Dempsey's coach strangely told him to lose weight, even though he weighed no more than he did his first two years with the Saints. Dempsey was confused, and then suddenly was cut from the team. But he did not give up. He practiced kicking in a park at night and was signed soon after by the Philadelphia Eagles. By leading the NFL in field goal accuracy in 1971, Dempsey showed the Saints they had made a mistake. Four years later, he was traded to the Los Angeles Rams, where he made 21 of 26 field goals. He also played for the Houston Oilers and Buffalo Bills before retiring in 1979. For a man who had a stubbed arm and half a foot, Dempsey was not known for what he looked like but what he did. "It's been good for me through the years," he said many years later about his record-breaking kick. "People remember you."[2]

TOM DEMPSEY

SPORT: Football.

BORN: January 12, 1947, Milwaukee, Wisconsin.

COLLEGE: Palomar Junior College, San Diego, California.

PRO: New Orleans Saints, 1969–1970; Philadelphia Eagles,
    1971–1974; Los Angeles Rams, 1975–1976; Houston Oilers,
    1977; Buffalo Bills, 1978–1979.

STATS: Shares the record for the longest field goal in NFL history
    (63 yards), 1970.

HONORS: Pro Bowl, 1969.

Tom Dempsey led the NFL in field goal accuracy in 1971, when he
played for the Philadelphia Eagles. Four years later, he made 21 of
26 field goals with the Los Angeles Rams.

Internet Address

http://www.sportsline.com/u/football/nfl/legends/ltatdempsey.htm

PETE GRAY

IT WAS THE SPRING OF 1945. America and the Allies were trying to win World War II. President Franklin Roosevelt had ordered Major League Baseball to continue during the war to boost morale. Few inspired America's sports fans and wounded veterans returning from overseas more than Pete Gray.

Gray played outfield for the American League's St. Louis Browns. (The Browns would later move to Baltimore and become the Orioles.) In the minor leagues a year earlier, Gray had smacked 5 homers and tied the Southern Association record for steals with 68. Gray did not have as good a season with the Browns in 1945. He managed just a .218 batting average with 6 doubles and 5 stolen bases the whole season. Yet each time Gray got a hit or made a catch, everyone marveled at his amazing skill. Why? Because Pete Gray had just one arm.

He was born Peter J. Wyshner in the coal-mining town of Nanticoke, Pennsylvania. His father labored as a coal miner, barely earning enough money to provide food for his wife and five children. As a boy, Gray dreamed of someday playing major-league baseball and taking care of his parents. But when he was six, his dream appeared shattered in a ghastly accident. His right arm was smashed beneath the wheel of a milk truck, and doctors were forced to cut it off at the shoulder.

Gray had to learn to use a knife and fork, tie his shoes, and do everything else with just one hand. Realizing that he could function normally with one arm, he thought that maybe he could play baseball, too. He taught himself to hit

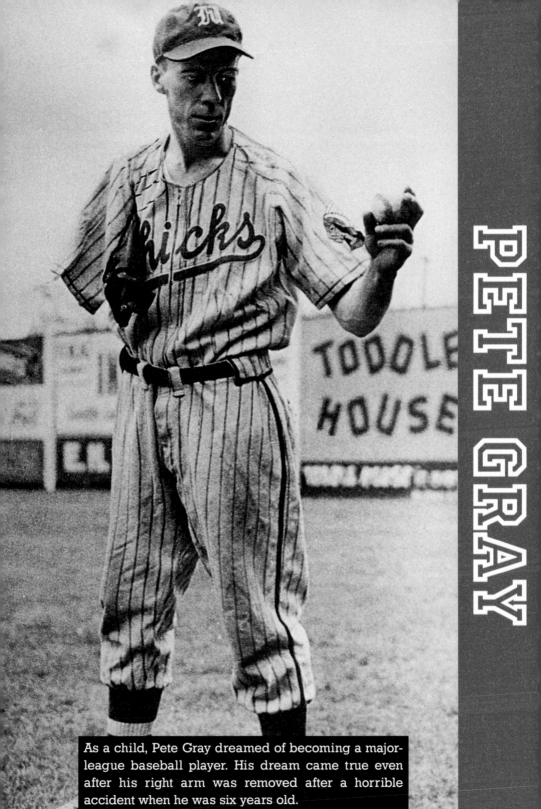

PETE GRAY

As a child, Pete Gray dreamed of becoming a major-league baseball player. His dream came true even after his right arm was removed after a horrible accident when he was six years old.

one-handed by tossing rocks into the air and hitting them with a stick, and, later, with a bat. He learned to catch and throw by pinning his glove and the ball to his chest, slipping off his glove, then gripping the ball to throw it, all in one quick motion. He became so skilled that in 1940 the local semipro Hanover Pitt team signed him as an outfielder.

Gray sent a letter one day to New York Giants manager Mel Ott, asking for a tryout. Ott agreed and invited him to Miami for spring training. But when Gray arrived and Ott saw that he had only one arm, he shook his head and said, "I'm sorry, kid. But it's tough enough for a man with two arms to play major-league ball."[1]

Gray did not give up on his dream. In 1943, he joined the Quebec club of the Canadian-American League and hit a grand slam in his first at-bat. The next year he was signed by the minor-league Memphis Chicks where he batted .333, knocked in 68 runs, and earned the league's Most Valuable Player award. He became a national hero and was flooded with requests to appear at public functions. He was embarrassed by all the attention. He just wanted to play baseball.

Then Gray got the call he had dreamed about. Luke Sewell, manager of the St. Louis Browns, invited Gray to join his team. Fans from everywhere came to see the one-armed player in the gray wool uniform. New York sportswriters dubbed him the "one-armed wonder." He played only one year in the major leagues, and some say he never would have made it at all if so many regular players hadn't been in the armed forces fighting overseas. When the war ended, he went back to the minors, where he played until 1949. Then he returned to his quiet Pennsylvania hometown where he lived in private. He declined to grant interviews, and to ensure his privacy, he did not even own a telephone. "I don't want to be bothered, that's all," he said.[2]

PETE GRAY

SPORT: Baseball.

BORN: March 6, 1915, Nanticoke, Pennsylvania.

PRO: St. Louis Browns, 1945.

STATS: Tied Southern Association single-season record for steals with 68 in 1944.

HONORS: Southern Association Most Valuable Player, 1944.

Although Pete Gray played in the major leagues for only one year, his ability to play baseball with only one arm inspired many American sports fans and wounded World War II veterans.

Internet Address

http://www3.primary.net/~tdalton/stlbrowns/brplayrs.htm

BEN HOGAN

Ben Hogan won several prestigious golf tournaments, including the PGA championship, before he was seriously injured in a car accident.

BEN HOGAN

BEN HOGAN AND HIS WIFE, VALERIE, drove along the highway near El Paso, Texas, struggling to see the road through the thick fog. Suddenly they spotted an enormous bus coming right at them. Hogan hurled his body across the front seat to shield his wife from injury. Ben's side of the car was crushed. Luckily, his wife escaped serious injury. Ben did not. His collarbone, leg, and pelvis were broken, and his ribs were shattered. In the hospital he nearly died from blood clots that formed in his legs. Doctors said he would be lucky just to walk again. "Right now, he's fighting for his life," wrote a reporter. "But if he wins that battle, he won't play golf anymore."[1] That reporter did not know the will and determination of Ben Hogan.

William Ben Hogan was born in Dublin, Texas, as the third and last child of Chester and Clara Hogan. Chester Hogan was a blacksmith, but when Ben was nine, his father committed suicide with a handgun while Ben was in the room. Ben's mother moved her family to Fort Worth, where Ben took a job at age twelve as a caddie at the Glen Garden Country Club. He fell in love with the game, and at age seventeen he became a pro. For the next nine years he never won a tournament, and he nearly went bankrupt several times.

Yet Hogan was determined to succeed. He competed during the day and practiced his shots at night. He finally won his first tournament in 1938 at age twenty-seven, then won five times more the following year. He always seemed to finish among the leaders, taking second place a record eleven times in 1941. In 1946 he won his first major, the

PGA (Professional Golfers' Association) Championship, and in 1948 he won ten times.

Then on February 2, 1949, disaster struck. His car was crushed by a Greyhound bus. Before Hogan could swing a club again, first he had to learn to walk. He climbed from his hospital bed to the floor each day to shuffle in pain across the room. Slowly he regained his strength. Eleven months after the accident, Hogan miraculously returned to the tour. In June, he entered the prestigious U.S. Open at Merion Golf Club in Ardmore, Pennsylvania. The final two rounds were played on the same day. Hogan could barely walk eighteen holes. How would he ever walk thirty-six? Between rounds he soaked his legs in a tub and wrapped them in bandages. With seven holes to go and Hogan in the lead, his legs stiffened on a tee shot, and he nearly collapsed. He staggered to a golf official and grabbed hold, saying, "Let me hang on to you for a little bit. My God, I don't think I can finish. My legs have turned to stone."[2] As fans applauded his courage, he limped the rest of the way to finish in a tie. He returned the next day with bandaged legs to win the playoff.

Hogan won the Open again the following year, and in 1953 he won five of the six tournaments he entered, including three majors. He continued playing competitive golf until 1971, and at the end of the twentieth century his 63 victories still ranked third all-time behind Sam Snead and Jack Nicklaus.

BEN HOGAN

SPORT: Golf.

BORN: August 13, 1912, Dublin, Texas.

DIED: July 25, 1997.

TURNED PRO: 1929.

FIRST PRO VICTORY: Hershey Ball Four, 1938.

STATS: Tied record for most U.S. Open victories with 4; holds record for most victories in a season (10), 1948; ranks third in all-time victories with 63.

HONORS: PGA Hall of Fame; Golf Hall of Fame; World Golf Hall of Fame; PGA Player of the Year Award, 1948, 1950, 1951, and 1953.

Hogan nearly died from blood clots that formed in his legs after his accident. Although doctors told him he would never be able to play golf again, Hogan returned to the sport eleven months after the accident.

Internet Address

http://golfeurope.com/almanac/players/hogan.htm

JACKIE JOYNER-KERSEE

Refusing to allow asthma to hold her back, Jackie Joyner-Kersee started sprinting at age nine, and long jumping at twelve. In high school, she excelled in track and field, basketball, and volleyball.

JACKIE JOYNER-KERSEE

TEARS STREAMED DOWN JACKIE JOYNER'S FACE as she stood on the track at the Los Angeles Memorial Coliseum. The spectators at the 1984 Summer Olympics had just seen Joyner miss the gold medal by the blink of an eye. She had lost the 800 meters by six-one-hundredths of a second (.06), which is about the speed of a hand clap. Her score of 6,385 points in the grueling seven-event heptathlon was just five points short of the gold. But Joyner was not crying for herself. Her tears were of joy for her brother's stunning success. On another part of the field, Al Joyner had just shocked the sporting world by winning the gold medal in the triple jump. Jackie knew she would have more chances. She had overcome a breathing condition just to be there, and she knew she was capable of almost anything.

Jacqueline Joyner had grown up in poor East St. Louis, Illinois, alongside the Mississippi River. Her father, Alfred, worked as a railroad switchman, and her mother, Mary, was a nurse's assistant. The family had little money. Jackie's brother, Al, said, "I remember Jackie and me crying together in a back room in that house, swearing that someday we were going to make it. Make it out. Make things different."[1]

Joyner-Kersee suffered from an ailment called asthma, which affects the respiratory system by constricting airflow into the lungs. When she was nine, she saw a sign one day at the local community center advertising a new track program. She joined the next competition and lost every race. But soon she began winning sprint races such as the 100-yard, 220-yard, and 440-yard events. At age twelve she started long jumping. At age fourteen she won her first heptathlon.

Though she sometimes wheezed and coughed after a race, she refused to allow her asthma to hold her back.

In high school she became an All-City star in basketball, volleyball, and track. A fine student, she graduated in the top 10 percent of her class. She won an athletic scholarship to UCLA to compete in basketball and track. She set several team records in basketball, but track was her main focus. Bruins coach Bob Kersee, whom she later married, encouraged her to focus on the heptathlon. He taught her to throw the shot (a metal ball) and the javelin (a long spear). In the heptathlon, athletes amass points in seven events spread out over two days. On the first day, the athletes compete in the 100-meter high hurdles, high jump, shot put, and 200-meter dash. The long jump, javelin throw, and 800-meter run are held on the second day.

Joyner finished second in the heptathlon in the 1984 Olympics when she was just twenty-two-years-old. Then she won the next nine heptathlons she entered. She set a new world record at the 1986 Goodwill Games, becoming the first woman to break the 7,000-point barrier. She broke the world record three more times, including a gold-medal score of 7,291 at the 1988 Olympic Games. Also at the 1988 Games she became the first American ever to win a gold medal in the long jump. She and running star Florence Griffith became friends, and Joyner's brother, Al, married Griffith, who changed her name to Florence Griffith-Joyner.

Joyner-Kersee won another gold at the 1992 Olympics, and by that time she had made herself and the heptathlon famous. She is widely considered the greatest multi-event athlete in women's track history. She helped make it cool for girls to compete hard at sports, though she is too humble to accept any credit. "All I ever wanted was to be able to compete," she said. "I don't take credit, because people came before me."[2]

JACKIE JOYNER-KERSEE

SPORT: Track and field.

BORN: March 3, 1962, East St. Louis, Illinois.

HIGH SCHOOL: Lincoln High School, East St. Louis, Illinois.

COLLEGE: UCLA.

ACHIEVEMENTS: Gold-medal winner, long jump, World Championships, 1987, 1991; gold-medal winner, long jump, 1988 Summer Olympics; bronze-medal winner, long jump, 1992 and 1996 Summer Olympics; gold-medal winner, heptathlon, 1988 and 1992 Summer Olympics; scored a world-record 7,291 points in the heptathlon at the Olympic Games, 1988.

HONORS: Broderick Cup (nation's top collegiate sportswoman), 1985; Sullivan Award (nation's best amateur athlete), 1986.

Joyner-Kersee won the silver medal in the heptathlon at the 1984 Olympics, and won gold medals in the same event in 1988 and 1992. She is considered by many to be the greatest multi-event athlete in the history of women's track and field.

Internet Address

http://www.usatf.org/athletes/bios/jjk.shtml

CASEY MARTIN

Despite suffering from Klippel-Trenaunay-Weber Syndrome in his right leg, Casey Martin won the first event he entered on the Nike Tour.

CASEY MARTIN

THE CHEERING WAS SO LOUD, so earsplitting, it was as if he had just made a long putt to win the U.S. Open. Instead, Casey Martin had simply been introduced by the course announcer at the first tee. A huge gallery of fans had amassed at San Francisco's prestigious Olympic Club for the 1998 Open to see Martin. They rose to their feet and applauded—those who could stand, anyway. The ones sitting yelled encouragement from their wheelchairs. Martin was not known for his great golf shots. In fact, not only had he never before won a PGA Tour event, he had never even *played* in one. Never hit a single shot. So why the big fuss?

Casey Martin suffers from a birth defect in his right leg known as Klippel-Trenaunay-Weber Syndrome. It is a disease in which the blood does not circulate properly in his leg. His leg is withered and weak, and too much walking could shatter it at any moment. It is only a matter of time, doctors say, until the leg does break, and when that happens it will likely have to be amputated. "I only have so many steps left in it," said Martin.[1]

Casey Martin was born in Eugene, Oregon, where he tried to keep up with his older brother at sports, learned to play the piano, studied hard, and fell in love with golf. He earned a scholarship to Stanford University, where he played with Tiger Woods and became a top-flight player. In college his disability worsened to the point that in order to walk on the golf course he had to wear two leg-long support stockings to keep his leg from swelling. It ached every minute he was on it, and he even had trouble sleeping at night.

In 1997 he inched closer to his dream of becoming a pro golfer when he finished eleventh at the PGA Tour Qualifying Tournament. This allowed him to compete on the Nike Tour, which was originally called the Hogan Tour, named after Ben Hogan, another disabled golfer. Martin won the first tournament he entered, the Lakeland Classic, and earned $40,500 in prize money. His story suddenly became national news. A year earlier, the PGA had denied Martin the use of a motorized cart to ride along the fairways on the Nike Tour, saying it could give him an unfair advantage, and many pro golfers agreed. Tiger Woods wasn't sure. "As a friend I'd love to see him have a cart," said Woods. "But from a playing standpoint, is it an advantage? It could be."[2] Martin sued in court, saying a law called the Americans with Disabilities Act supported him. A judge agreed, allowing Martin to use a cart.

Was golf easier for Martin now? Apparently not. He finished tied for sixteenth in his next tournament, then thirteenth, then missed the cut twice in a row. In June he qualified to play at the U.S. Open, where he was hailed for his courage. "It was overwhelming," Martin said. "I have to admit I was almost crying on the first tee. I had to get up there and hit it quick."[3]

With people in wheelchairs following him around the hilly course, Martin shot rounds of 74, 71, 74, and 72, to finish tied for twenty-third. For his efforts, he took home $34,043. He had reached his dream of playing in a PGA Tour event, and he has played in several more since. Now Martin has bigger dreams. "I'd love to be known as a great golfer," he says. "Not as a guy in a cart or with a disability. Just a great golfer."[4]

CASEY MARTIN

SPORT: Golf.

BORN: June 2, 1972, Eugene, Oregon.

COLLEGE: Stanford University, Stanford, California.

TURNED PRO: 1995.

STATS: Shot holes-in-one in back-to-back rounds at the Oregon Open, 1994.

HONORS: Second-team All-America, 1994; Academic All-America, 1995.

The PGA denied Martin the use of a motorized cart on the Nike Tour, saying it could give him an unfair advantage over other golfers. Martin sued, and a judge, citing the Americans with Disabilities Act, supported him.

Internet Address

http://www.thehartford.com/corporate/special/casey.html

WILMA RUDOLPH

WILMA RUDOLPH LOOKED OUT THE WINDOW of the airplane at the blue Pacific Ocean far below and suddenly realized her situation. Here she was, just sixteen years old, on her way to Australia to compete in the Olympic Games. When she was younger, she had suffered from polio, a terrible sickness, and had been unable to walk without braces on her legs. "Is this all one big dream?" Rudolph asked herself. "It was only a couple of years ago that I couldn't even walk right, much less run. . . . Now here I was on this big chartered jet going off to another country as one of the fastest women in the whole world."[1]

Rudolph won a bronze medal at those 1956 Olympics as part of the American 4 x 100-meter relay team. But it is what she did four years later at the next Olympic Games that was truly remarkable, something for which she would become known as the "World's Fastest Woman."

Wilma Glodean Rudolph was born two months premature and weighed just four and a half pounds, the twentieth of twenty-two children born to Ed and Blanche Rudolph. Ed worked as a railroad porter, and Blanche did household chores for other families. The Rudolph family was poor, and Wilma wore clothes that her mother made from flour sacks. At age four, she contracted pneumonia, which infected her lungs and made it a struggle to breathe. She also developed scarlet fever, which is a disease that can damage the heart. Next she contracted polio, which is a virus that attacks the nerves. Her illnesses paralyzed her left leg. For the next four years, she limped with a heavy brace and was teased by other children at school. "I was so lonely, and I

WILMA RUDOLPH

Wilma Rudolph became known as the World's Fastest Woman after winning three track and field gold medals at the 1960 Olympics.

felt rejected," she said. "I would . . . close my eyes, and just drift off into a sinking feeling, going down, down, down. I cried a lot."[2]

Wilma Rudolph's parents massaged her leg daily, and her mother took her twice a week by bus to a hospital fifty miles away for treatment. She wore a special shoe until age eleven, when her mother decided one day to mail it back to the hospital. Blanche Rudolph believed that her daughter was well enough to wear a regular shoe. Wilma was so overjoyed that she wanted to spend every waking hour running and jumping. She joined her junior high school track team, where her coach nicknamed her Skeeter because she buzzed around like a mosquito.

Rudolph set a Tennessee state high school basketball scoring record with 49 points in a game, and in track she was so fast she managed to qualify for the 1956 Olympics. Four years later, in Rome, Italy, she became the first American woman to win three gold medals at an Olympic Games. She won the 100-meter dash in a world-record-setting 11 seconds flat, faster than any other woman in history. Then she won the 200-meter dash. Finally, she teamed with three others to win the 4 x 100-meter relay. She was swarmed on the field by adoring athletes and fans, then pulled to safety by officials who told her that her life would never be the same.

When the Olympics ended, she was invited to the Vatican to meet Pope John XXIII, then to the White House to meet President John F. Kennedy. She retired from competition soon after to travel around the country teaching poor children the value of sports and hard work. She enjoyed children so much that she became an elementary school teacher. In 1981 she started the Wilma Rudolph Foundation, which helps children to read and provides them with books about American heroes. Her autobiography, *Wilma*, should be at the top of the list.

WILMA RUDOLPH

SPORT: Track and field.

BORN: June 23, 1940, St. Bethelhem, Tennessee.

DIED: November 12, 1994.

HIGH SCHOOL: Burt High School, Clarksville, Tennessee.

COLLEGE: Tennessee State University.

STATS: Bronze-medal winner, 4 x 100-meter relay, 1956 Summer Olympics; gold-medal winner, 100-meter dash, 1960 Summer Olympics; gold-medal winner, 200-meter dash, 1960 Summer Olympics; gold-medal winner, 4 x 100-meter relay, 1960 Summer Olympics.

HONORS: Associated Press Female Athlete of the Year, 1960, 1961; Sullivan Award winner, 1961; inducted into National Track and Field Hall of Fame, 1974; inducted into the International Women's Sports Hall of Fame, 1980; Black Athletes Hall of Fame; inducted into the United States Olympic Hall of Fame, 1983.

In 1981, Rudolph started the Wilma Rudolph Foundation, which helps teach young children to read.

Internet Address

http://www.usatf.org/athletes/hof/rudolph.shtml

KENNY WALKER

Though hearing impaired, Kenny Walker is said to have been the best listener on his team. By reading his teammates' lips in the huddle, he never missed his

KENNY WALKER

THE NOISE THUNDERED SO LOUDLY in Rich Stadium in Buffalo, New York, that Kenny Walker could feel his shoulder pads vibrate. Walker's Denver Broncos had just taken the field for the 1992 AFC (American Football Conference) Championship Game against the Bills. "Our biggest concern is the noise. We have to be able to play in the noise," said Broncos assistant coach Marvin Bass. "And then there's Kenny Walker. Noise won't bother him. Nothing will bother him. Nothing ever does."[1]

Football is a game of sounds. Collisions. Cheers. Whistles. Quarterbacks barking signals. Coaches screaming. The sounds of football are as bright as the sights. Except for Kenny Walker. He played football in silence. Kenny Walker is deaf.

Walker was born in Crane, Texas. At age two he suffered from an inflammation of his spinal cord, called spinal meningitis. By age four he had lost his hearing. That year, Kenny's mother moved the family to Denver, Colorado, because the public school system there had a program for hearing-impaired students. Kenny Walker lived eleven years in Denver before moving back to Texas as a sophomore, where he joined the Crane High School football team as a linebacker. He received all-state honors as a center in basketball, and also starred on the track team. He earned a football scholarship to the University of Nebraska, where he made friends easily. Among them was future All-Pro lineman Neil Smith, who said, "Kenny could read lips from a mile away. I would come up to him and start talking nonsense. He would look at me for a minute, then shout, 'That ain't no word! Get out of my face.'"[2]

In four years at Nebraska, Walker developed into a powerful defensive lineman whose hits were anything but silent. He was a consensus All-America pick and Big Eight Defensive Player of the Year as a senior, but few pro teams wanted to take a chance on him. It wasn't until the eighth round of the NFL draft that the Denver Broncos decided to pick him. And they chose him only after the player they picked in the first round, Walker's Nebraska teammate Mike Croel, put in a good word for him. For the Broncos, it turned out to be a sound choice.

Walker signed a one-year contract for $146,000, which is cheap for a pro football player, and he made the team. Soon he became a starter. He read captain Karl Mecklenburg's lips in the huddle for defensive instructions. When the Broncos called an audible (changed their alignment at the line of scrimmage), a player tapped Walker on a certain spot on his back to indicate where he should line up. Walker never missed an assignment. "I wish the rest of our players listened with as much attention as he does," said Coach Wade Phillips.[3]

Walker's courage inspired the Broncos to reach the AFC championship game his rookie year, and even though they lost, his teammates voted him the team's Most Inspirational Player. He started at defensive tackle again a year later, but the Broncos switched him to nose guard in 1993. Walker was unable to make the transition and was released. He joined the Canadian Football League's Calgary Stampeders, where he starred for two years. He retired in 1995, leaving a message for anyone who would listen. "People can be proud and be deaf," Walker said. "They shouldn't be ashamed of it."[4]

KENNY WALKER

SPORT: Football.

BORN: April 6, 1967, Crane, Texas.

HIGH SCHOOL: Crane High School, Crane, Texas.

COLLEGE: University of Nebraska.

PRO: Denver Broncos, 1991–1992; Calgary Stampeders (Canadian Football League), 1993–1994.

STATS: Ranked second with Stampeders for sacks in a season (9), 1994.

HONORS: First-team All-America, 1990; Big Eight Conference All-Academic Team, 1990; Big Eight Conference Defensive Player of the Year, 1990; Broncos Most Inspirational Player, 1991; Philadelphia Sportswriters' Association Most Courageous Athlete Award, 1992.

Kenny Walker, who lost his hearing by age four due to spinal meningitis, developed into a powerful defensive lineman at the University of Nebraska. He was drafted by the Denver Broncos, and was voted the team's Most Inspirational Player in 1991.

CHAPTER NOTES

Jim Abbott

    1. "Winning at Their Own Game," *Time*, October 10, 1988, p. 83.

    2. Personal interview with author, April 19, 1990.

Grover Cleveland Alexander

    1. Tom Seaver, *Great Moments in Baseball* (New York: Birch Lane Press, 1992), p. 85.

    2. Ibid.

    3. Lowell Reidenbaugh, *Cooperstown—Where Baseball's Legends Live Forever* (St. Louis: The Sporting News Publishing Company, 1983), p. 12.

    4. Anthony J. Connor, *Baseball—For the Love of It* (New York: Macmillan Publishing Co., 1982), p. 192.

Mordecai Brown

    1. Jonathan Fraser Light, *The Cultural Encyclopedia of Baseball* (Jefferson, N.C.: McFarland & Company, Inc., 1997), p. 125.

Tom Dempsey

    1. Jerry Green, "Dempsey's Kick Still a Marvel After 25 Years," *Detroit News*, November 8, 1995, p. 1.

    2. Ibid.

Pete Gray

    1. Hal Butler, *Sports Heroes Who Wouldn't Quit* (New York: Julian Messner, 1973), p. 24.

    2. Armen Keteyian, "Lights! Camera! Action!" in Charles Einstein, ed., *The Fireside Book of Baseball* (New York: Simon & Schuster, 1987), p. 213.

Ben Hogan

    1. Hal Butler, *Sports Heroes Who Wouldn't Quit* (New York: Julian Messner, 1973), p. 106.

    2. Robert Sommers, *Golf Anecdotes* (New York: Oxford University Press, 1995), p. 161.

Jackie Joyner-Kersee

    1. Louise Mooney, *Newsmakers 93—The People Behind Today's Headlines* (Detroit, Mich.: Gale Research, 1993), p. 225.

    2. Tim Layden, "Farewell to JJK," *Sports Illustrated*, August 3, 1998, p. 29.

Casey Martin

1. Rick Reilly, "Give Casey Martin a Lift," *Sports Illustrated*, February 9, 1998, p. 140.

2. Nick Charles, "Fairway or No Way," *People Weekly*, February 9, 1998, p. 48.

3. Tim Keown, "Olympic Crowd Embraces Martin, Cart and All," *San Francisco Chronicle*, June 19, 1998, p. 2.

4. Charles, p. 48.

Wilma Rudolph

1. Wilma Rudolph, *Wilma* (New York: Signet, 1977), p. 91.

2. Ibid., p. 18.

Kenny Walker

1. Steve Simmons, "Gutsy Bronco an Inspiration," *Toronto Sun*, January 8, 1992, p. 62.

2. Kent Pulliam, "Skepticism About Deaf Player Fades Amid Success," *Kansas City Star*, October 20, 1991, p. 1.

3. Simmons, p. 62.

4. Pulliam, p. 1.

INDEX